# modern jazz quartet

Arranged by Brent Edstrom

2 AFTERNOON IN PARIS

6 BAGS' GROOVE

10 BLUES IN A MINOR

20 BLUES IN H (B)

24 BLUESOLOGY

28 CONCORDE

32 CONNIE'S BLUES

15 DELAUNEY'S DILEMMA

36 DJANGO

40 ECHOES

50 THE GOLDEN STRIKER

56 LA RONDE

45 MILANO

62 THE QUEEN'S FANCY

68 REUNION BLUES

73 SKATING IN CENTRAL PARK

78 A SOCIAL CALL

88 TEARS FROM THE CHILDREN

92 TWO DEGREES EAST, THREE DEGREES WEST

83 VENDÔME

ISBN 978-1-4584-0522-7

HAL•LEONARD®
CORPORATION

7777 W. BLUEMOUND RD. P.O. BOX 13819 MILWAUKEE, WI 53213

Visit Hal Leonard Online at
**www.halleonard.com**

# AFTERNOON IN PARIS

By JOHN LEWIS

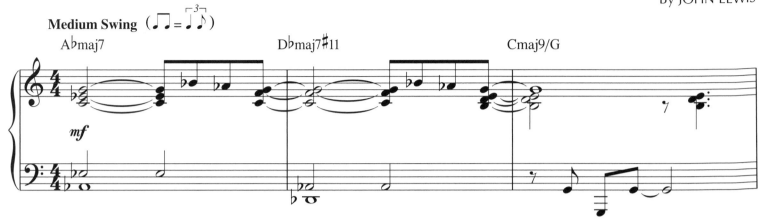

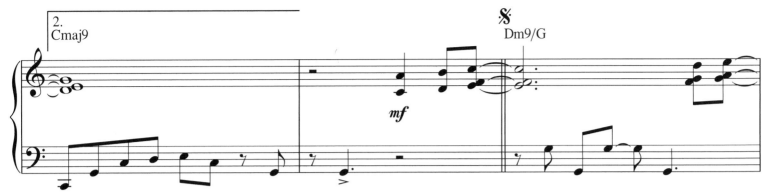

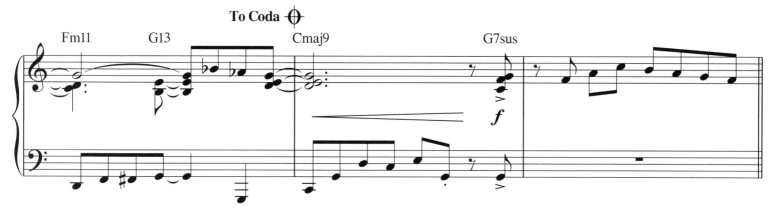

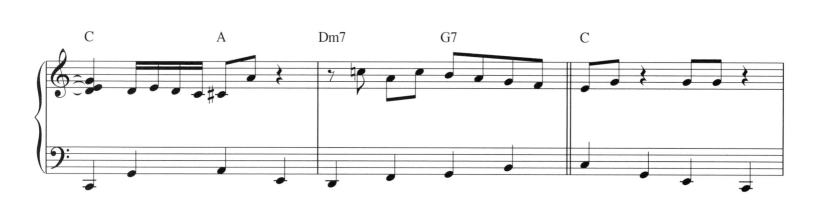

# BAGS' GROOVE

By MILT JACKSON

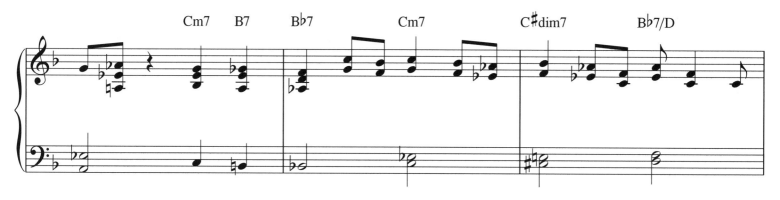

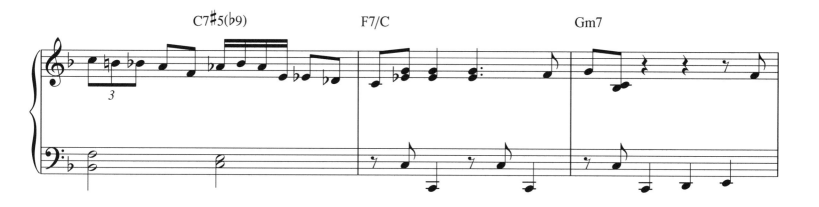

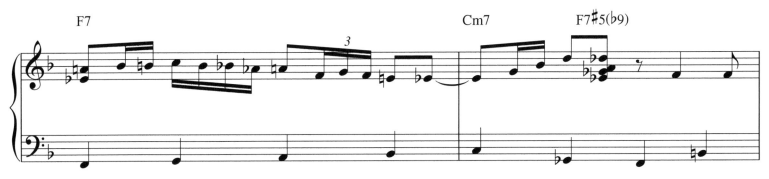

# BLUES IN A MINOR

By JOHN LEWIS

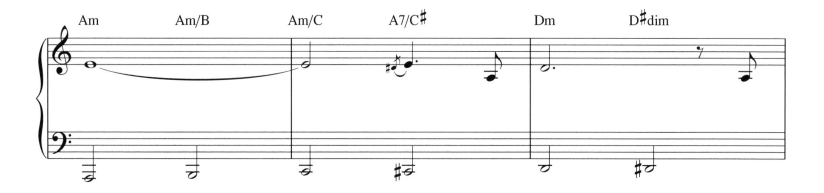

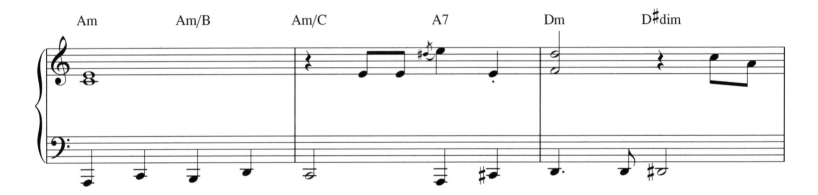

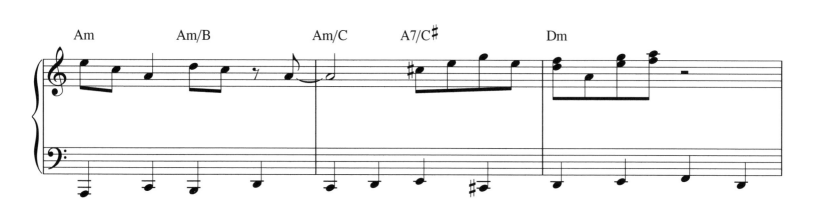

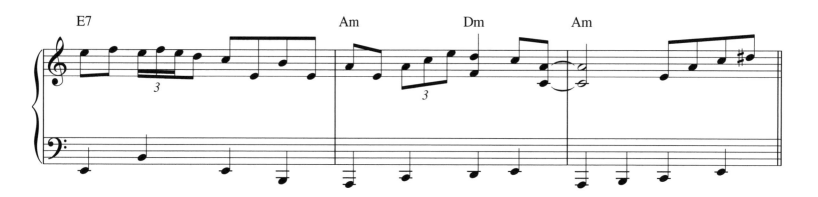

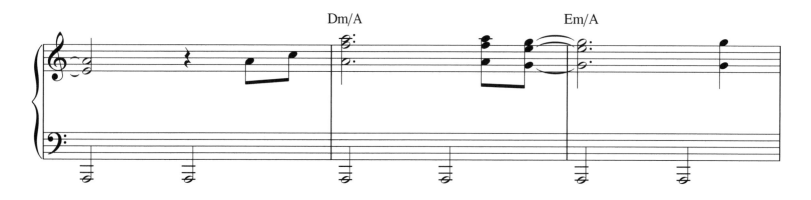

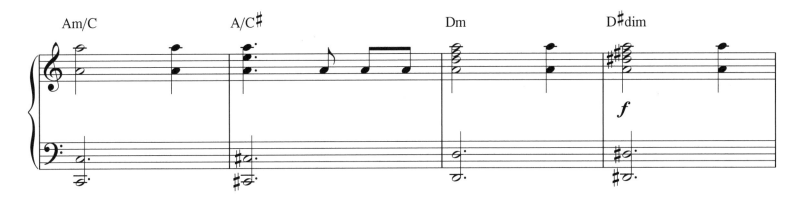

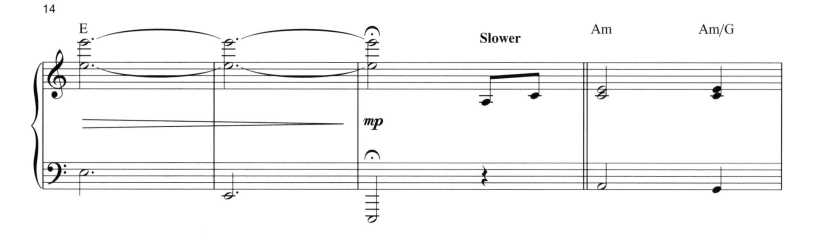

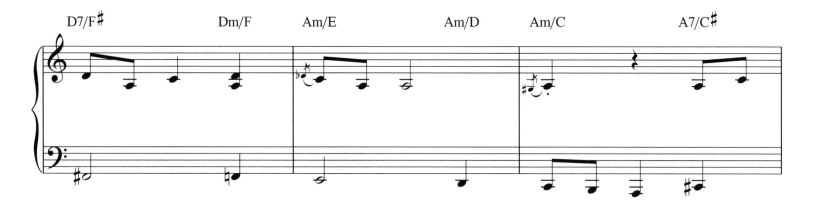

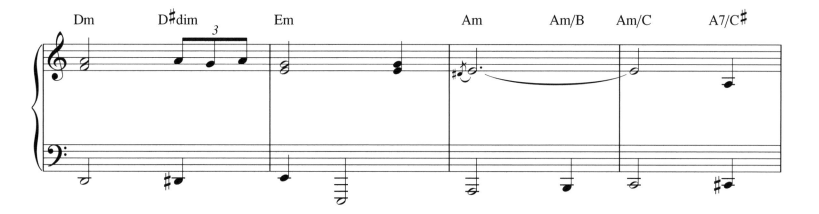

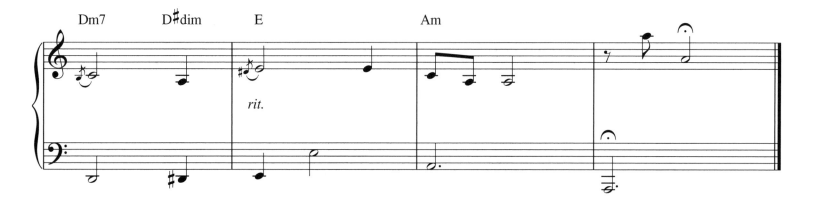

# DELAUNEY'S DILEMMA

By JOHN LEWIS

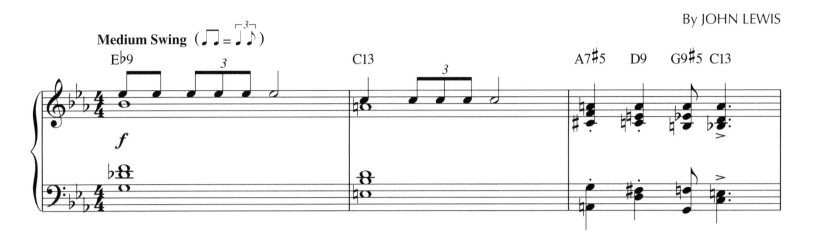

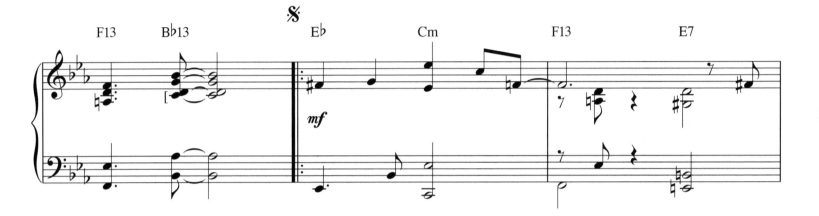

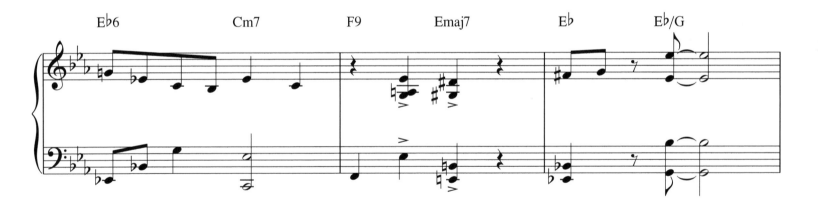

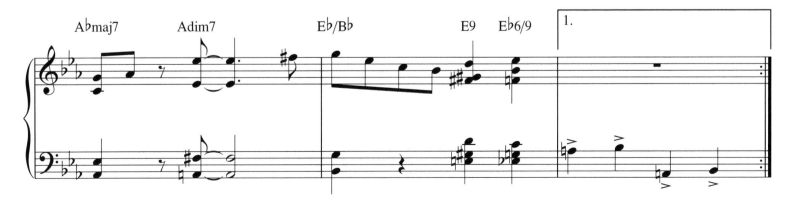

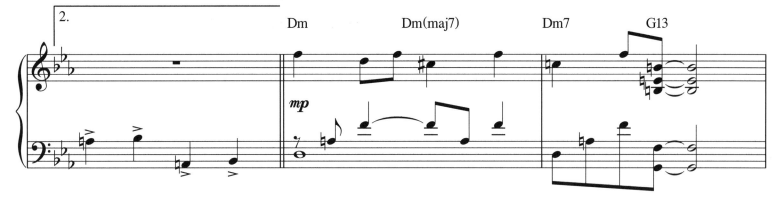

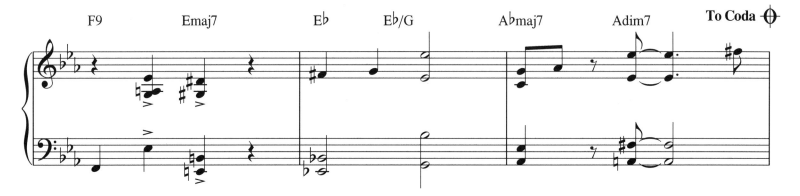

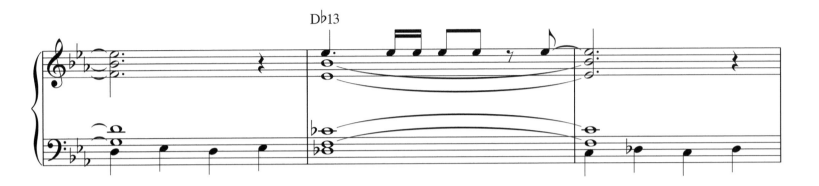

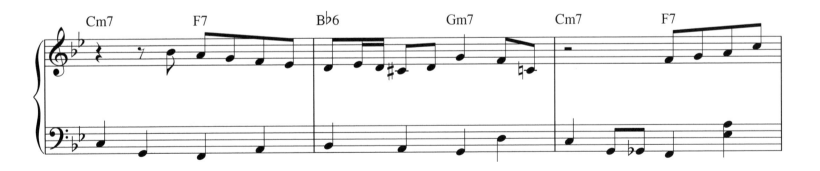

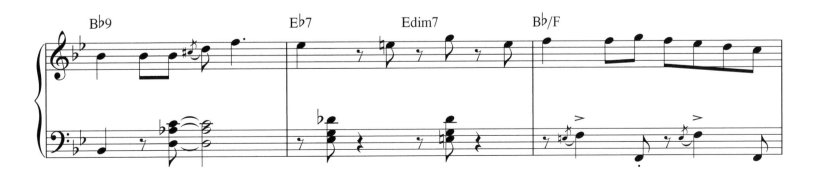

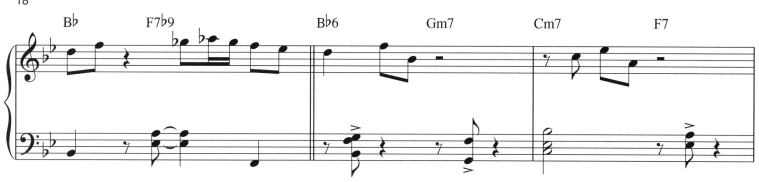

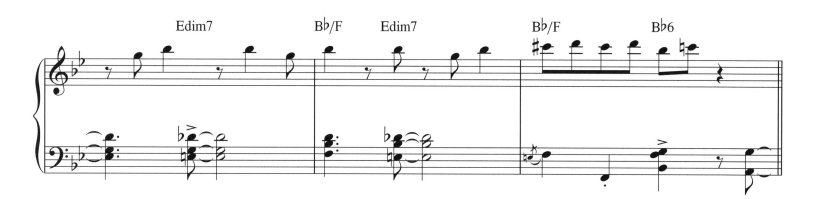

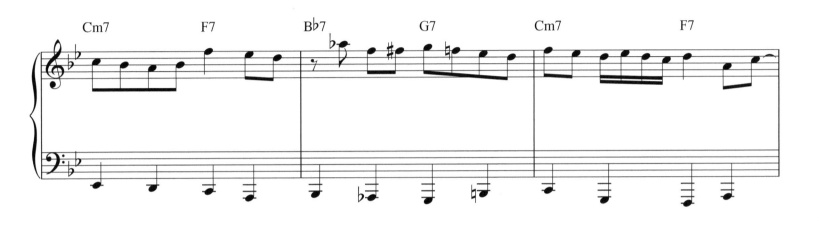

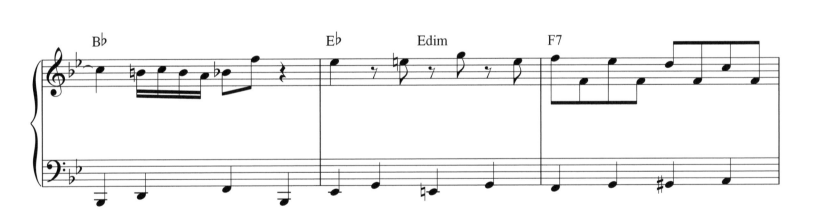

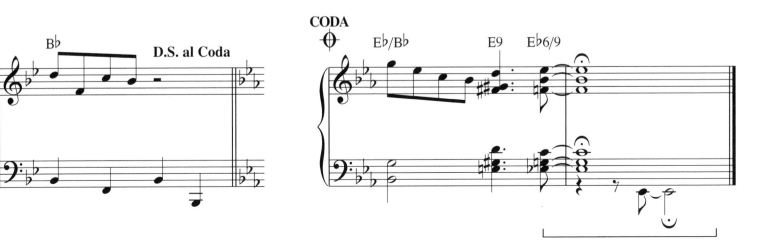

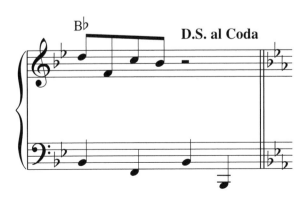

# BLUES IN H (B)

By MILT JACKSON

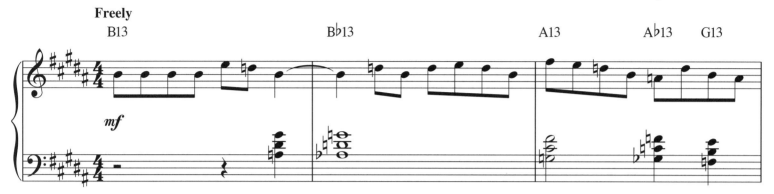

**To Coda**

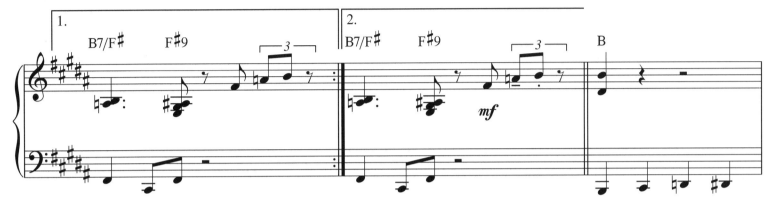

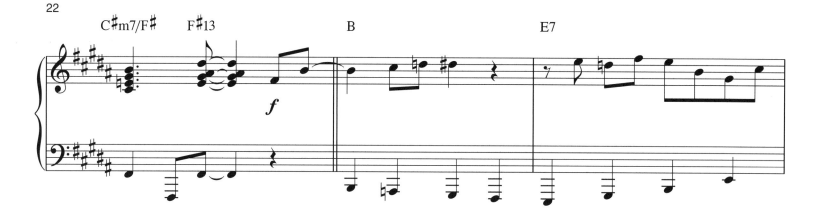

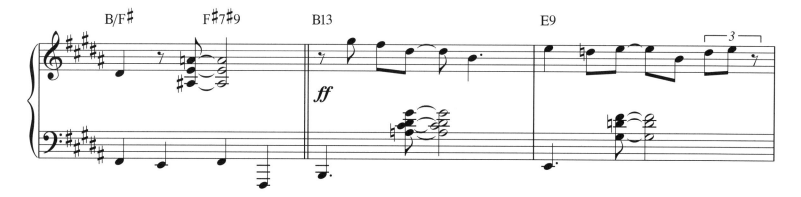

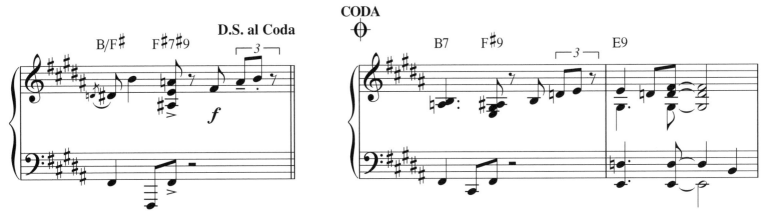

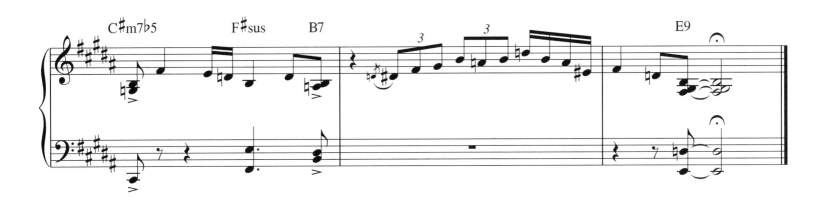

# BLUESOLOGY

By MILT JACKSON

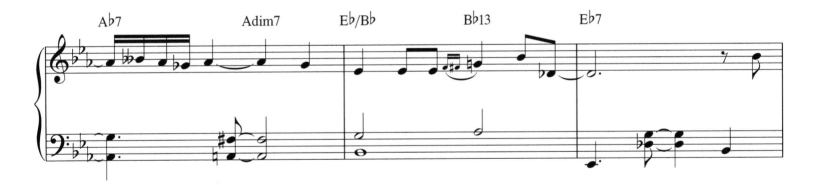

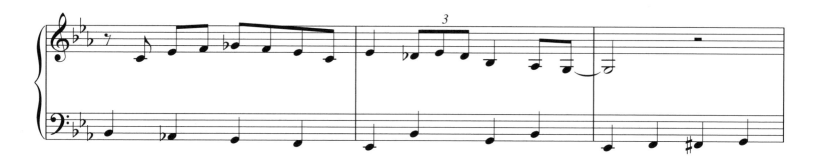

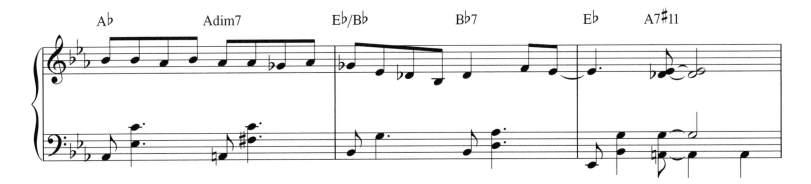

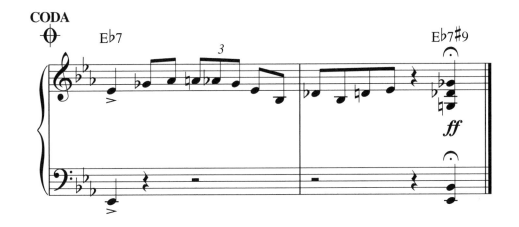

# CONCORDE

By JOHN LEWIS

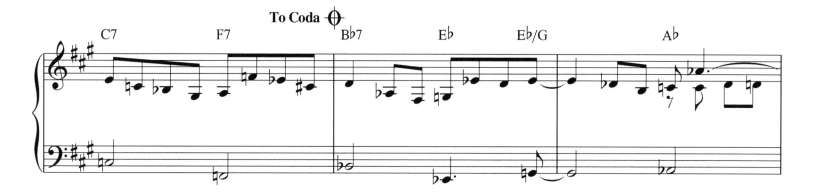

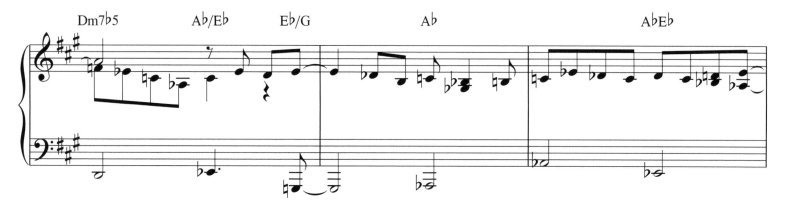

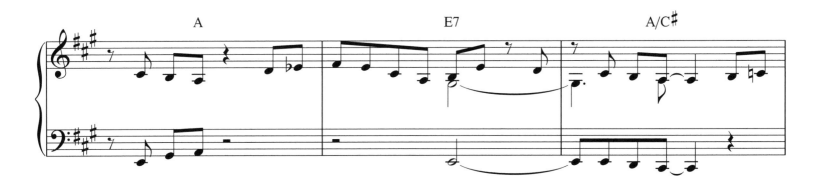

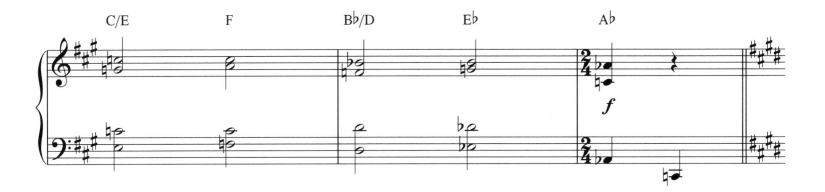

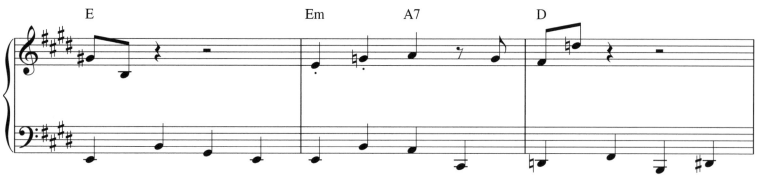

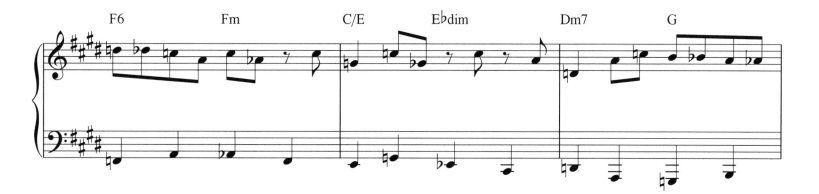

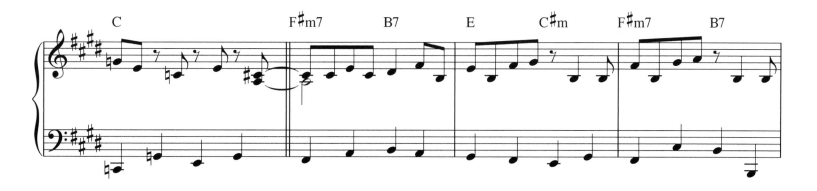

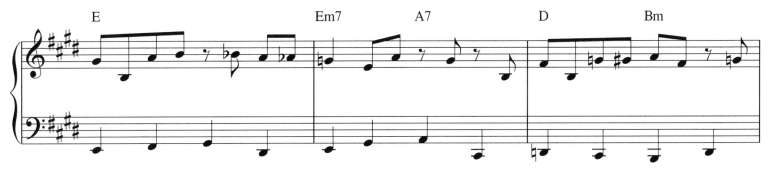

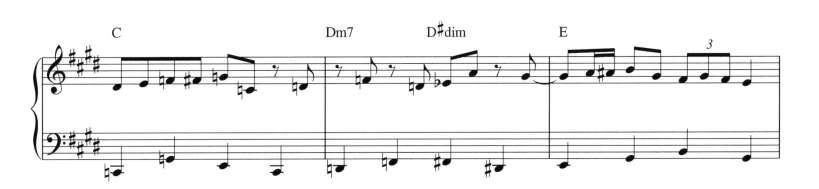

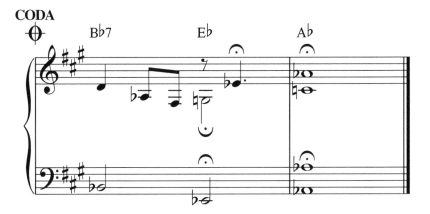

# CONNIE'S BLUES

By MILT JACKSON

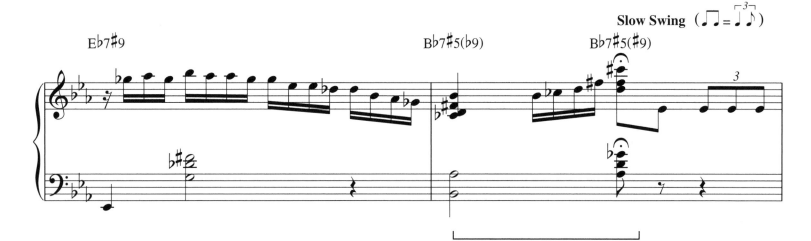

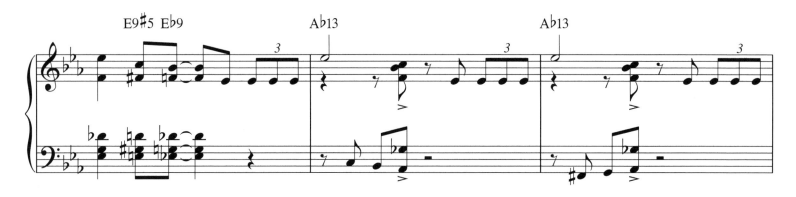

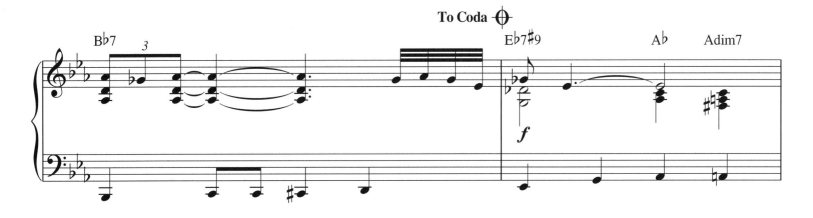

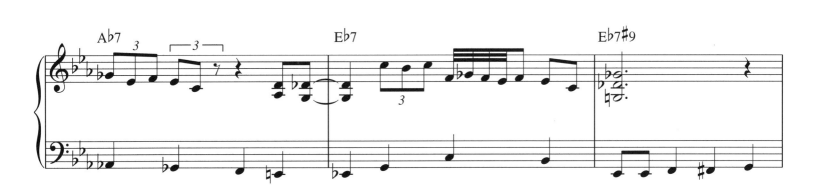

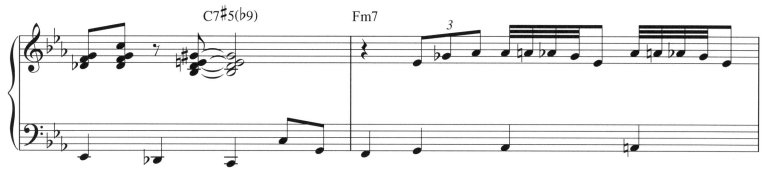

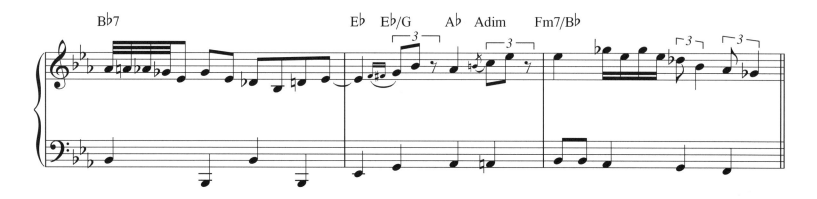

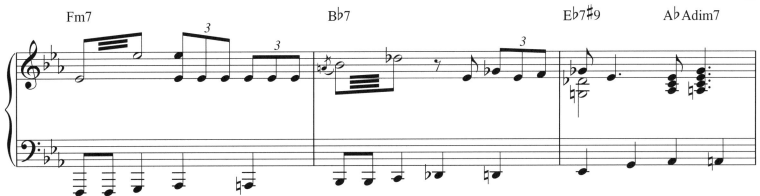

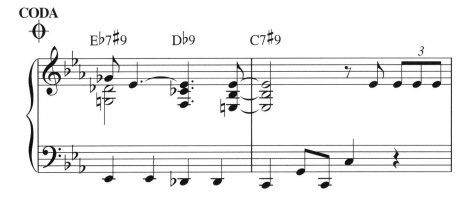

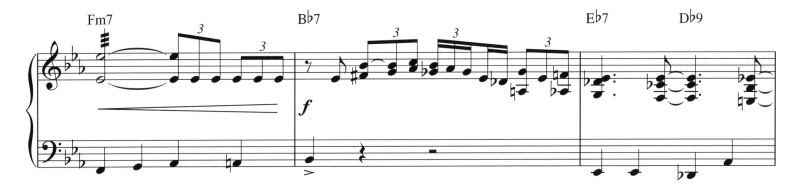

# DJANGO

By JOHN LEWIS

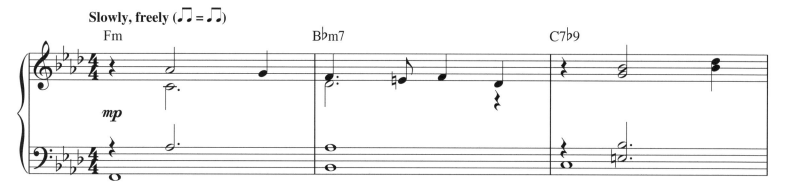

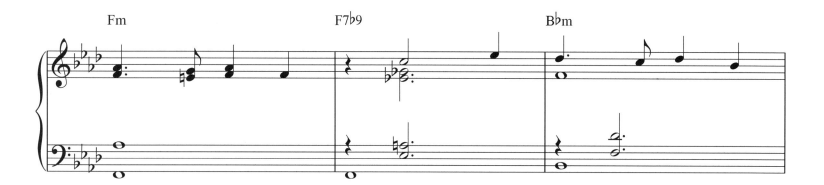

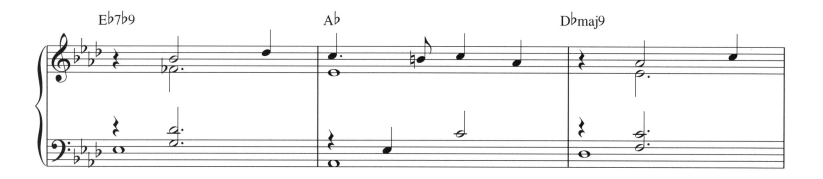

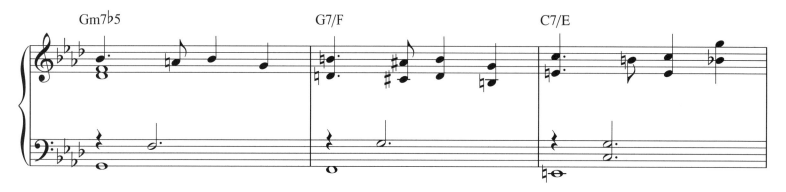

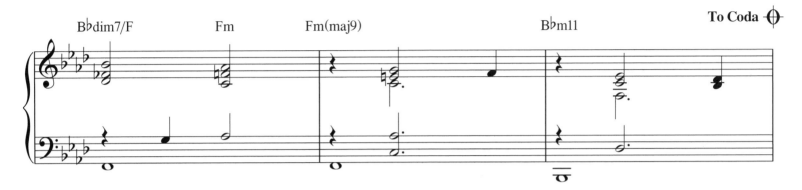

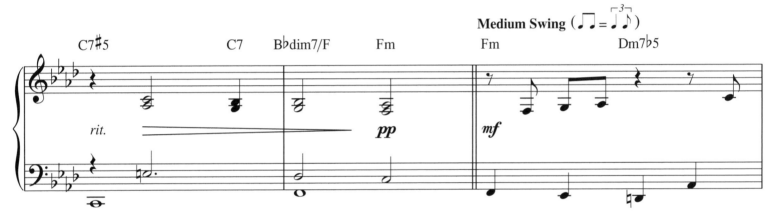

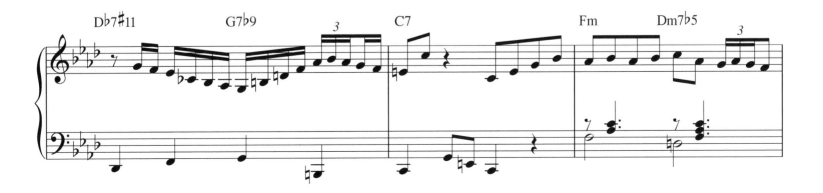

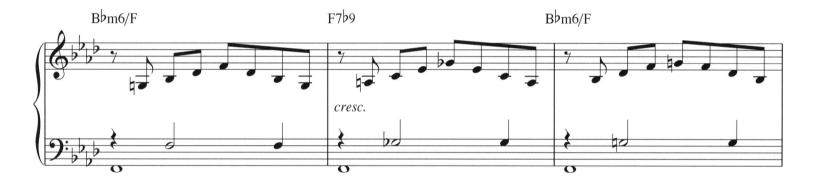

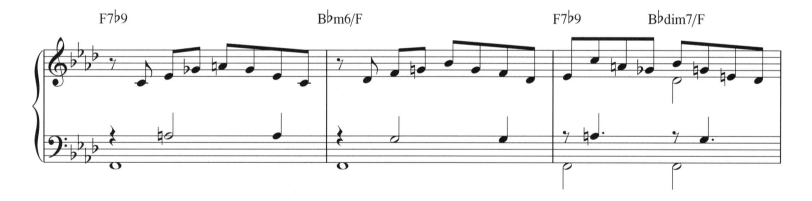

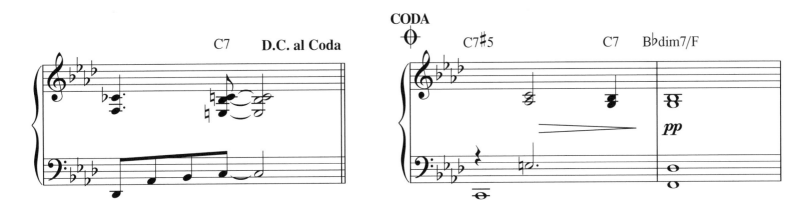

# ECHOES

By MILT JACKSON

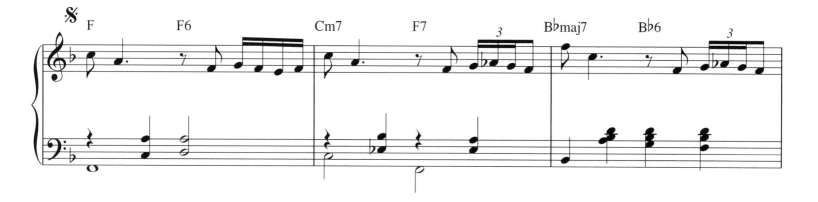

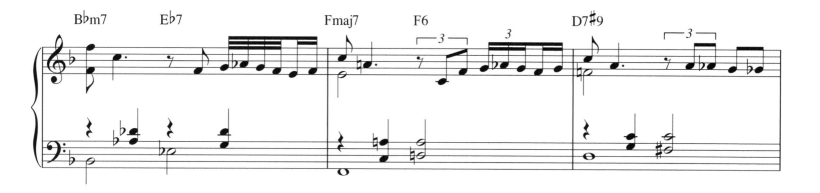

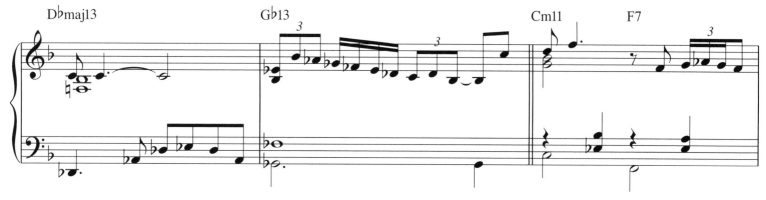

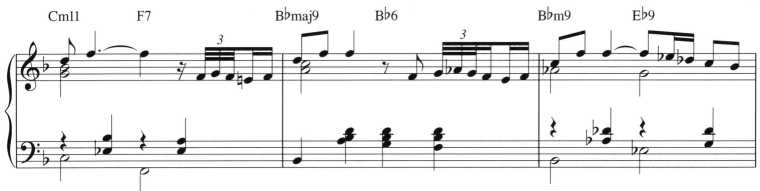

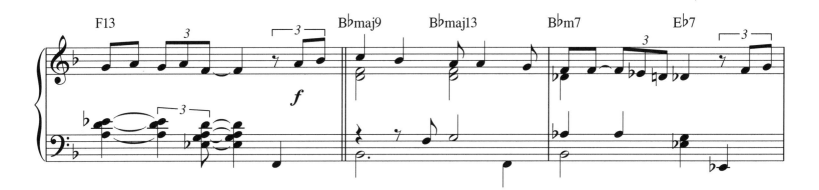

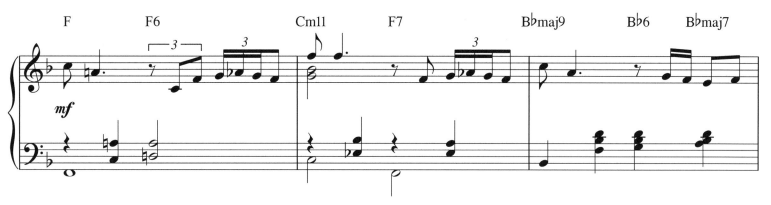

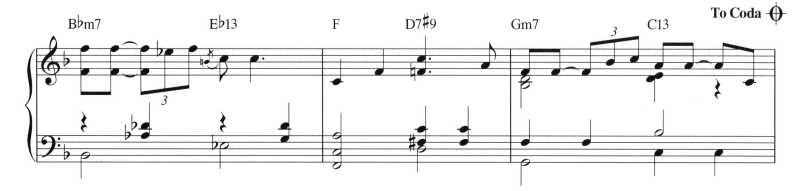

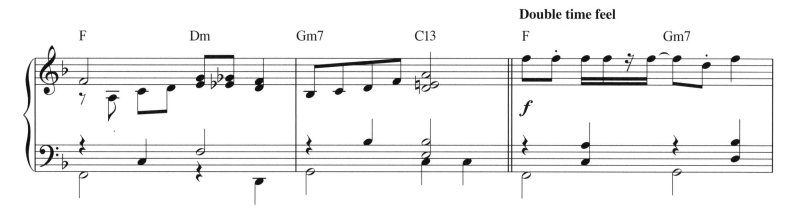

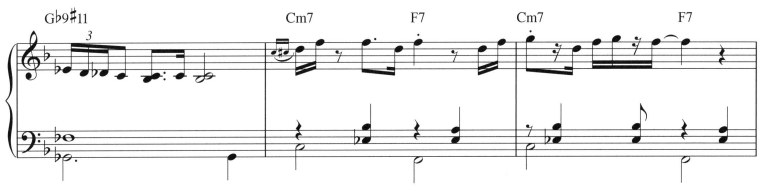

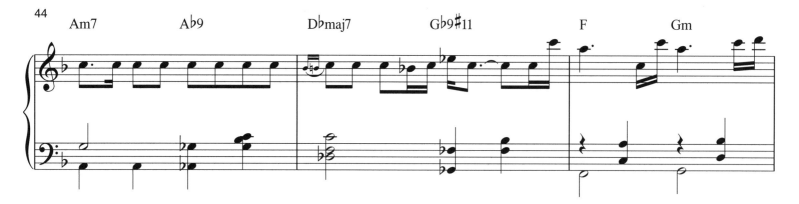

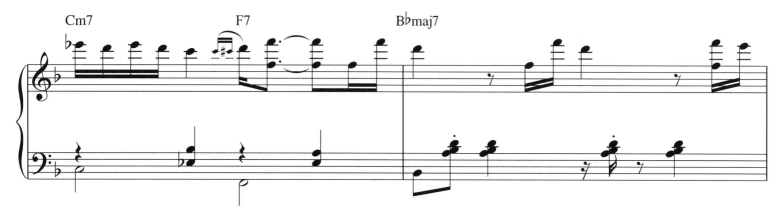

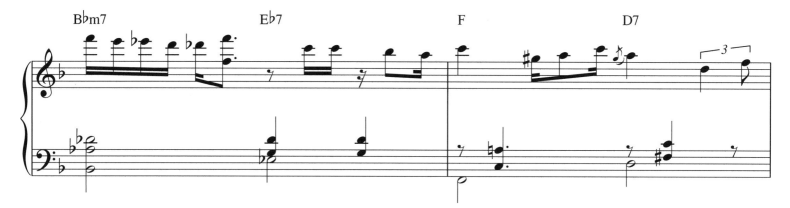

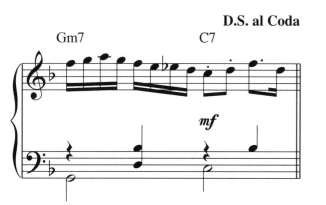

# MILANO

By JOHN LEWIS

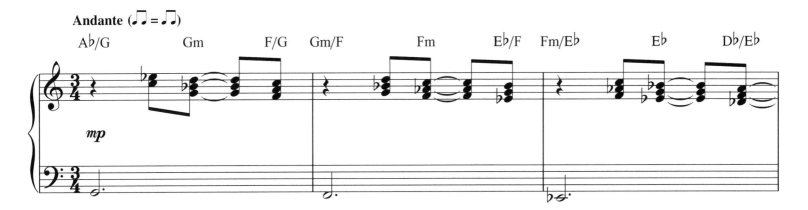

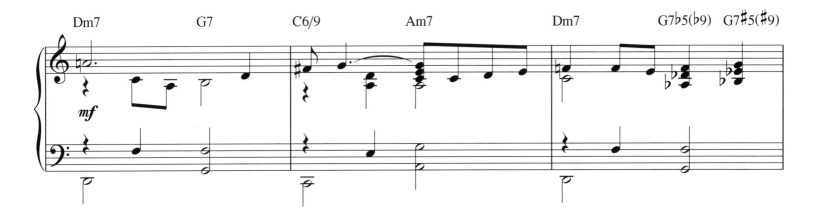

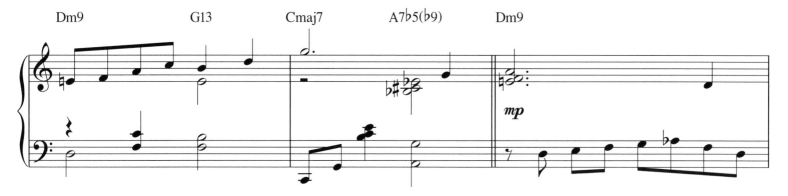

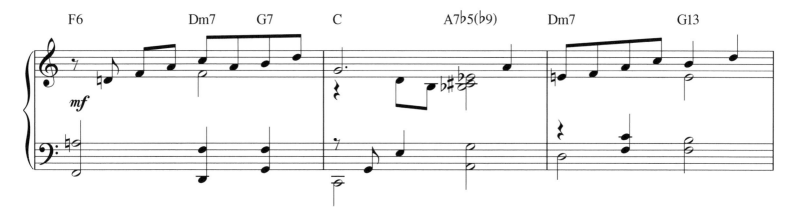

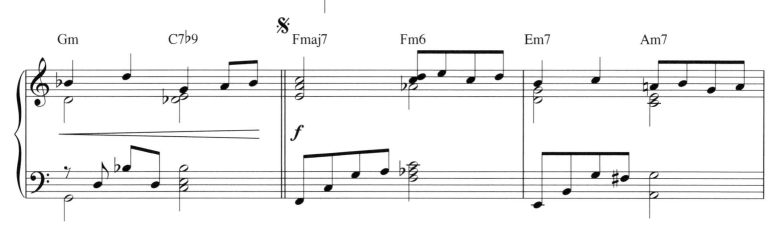

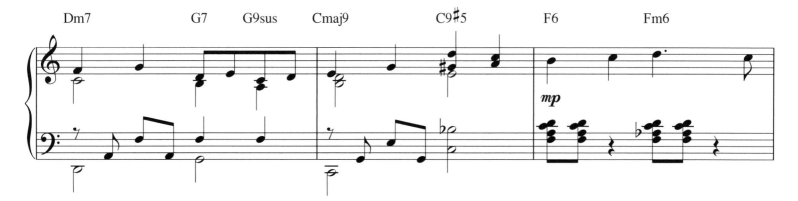

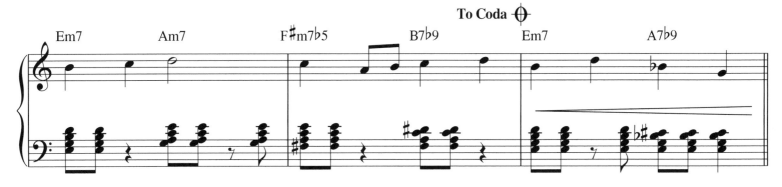

**Double-time Swing feel (until D.S.)**

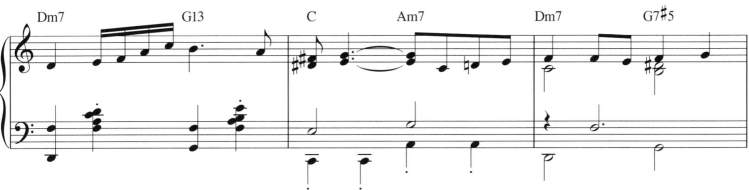

48

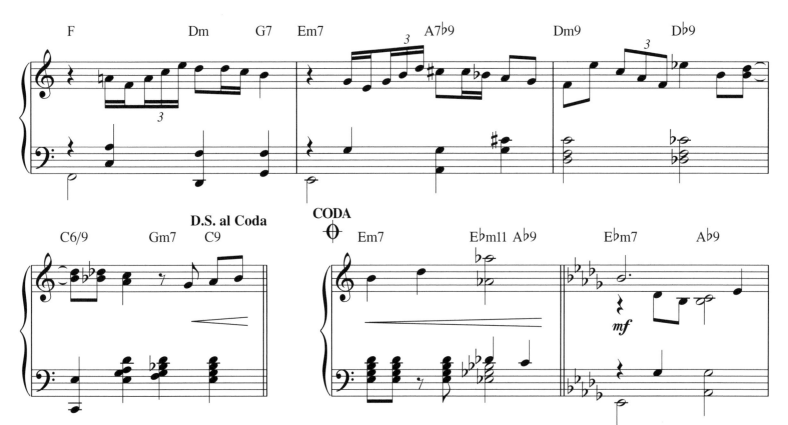

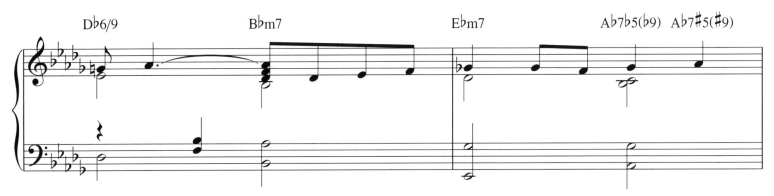

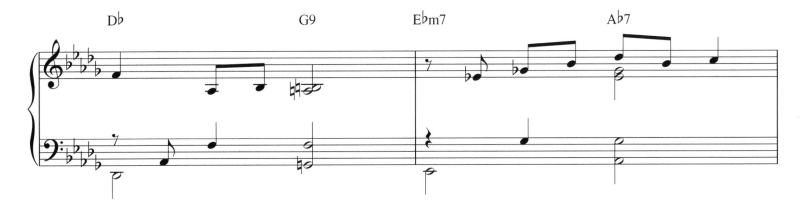

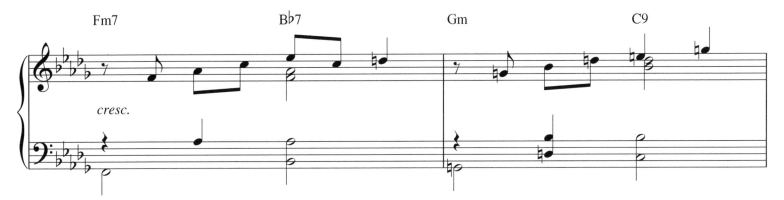

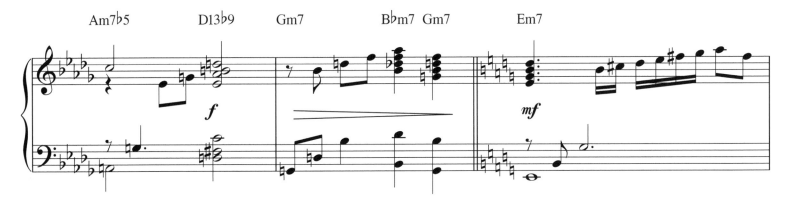

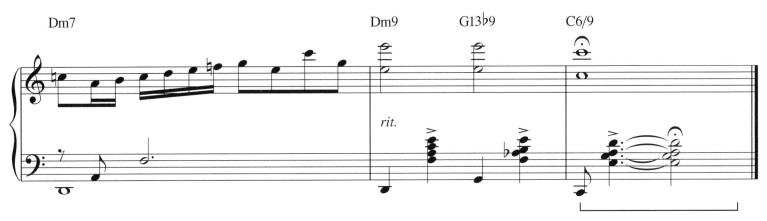

# THE GOLDEN STRIKER

By JOHN LEWIS

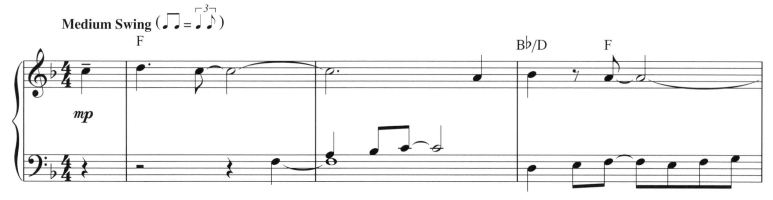

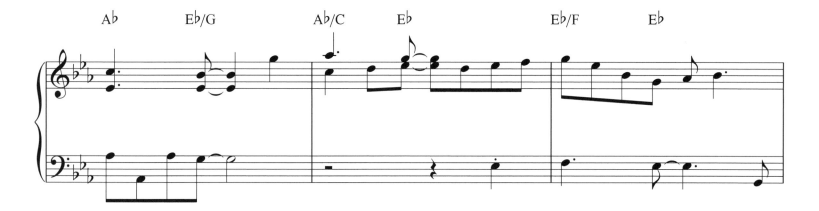

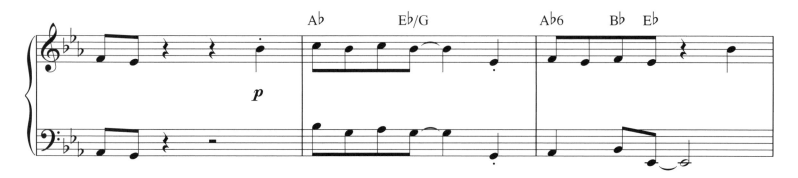

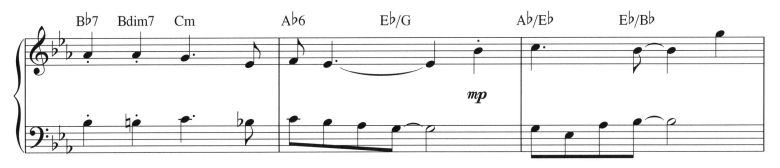

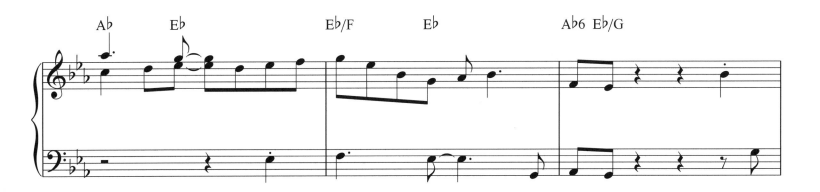

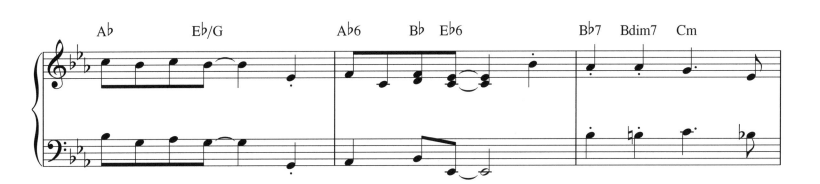

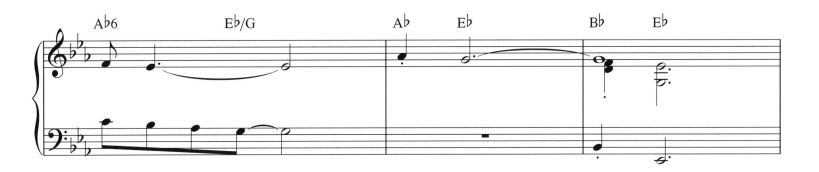

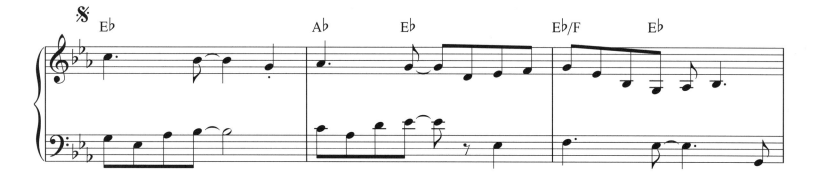

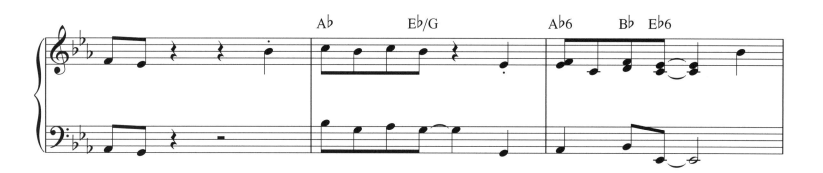

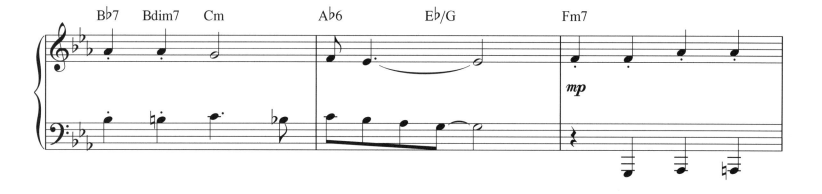

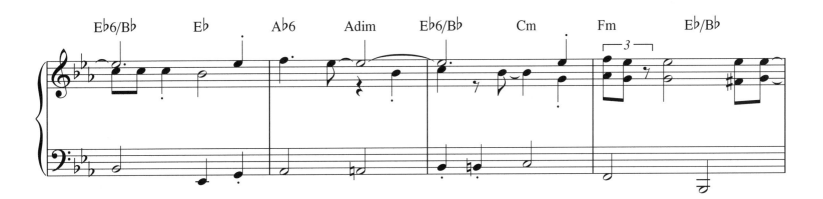

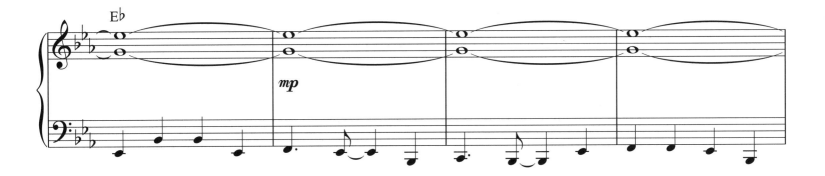

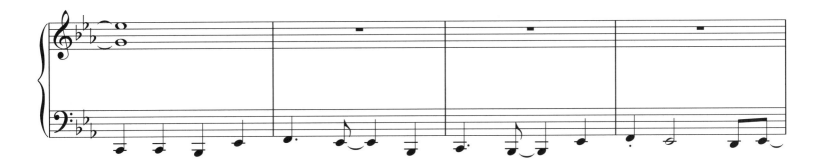

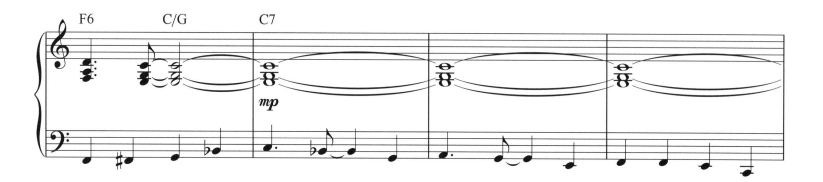

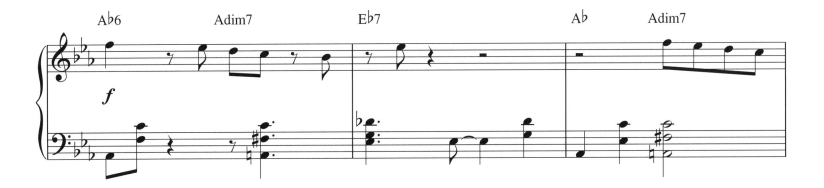

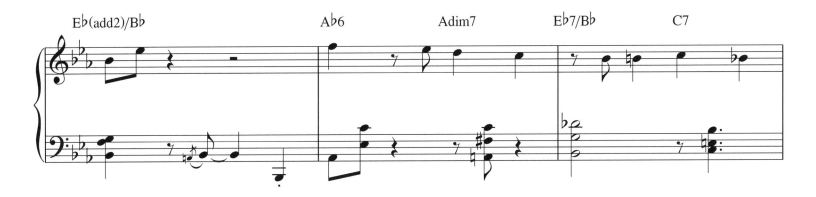

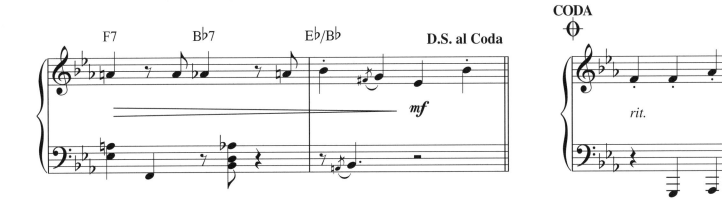

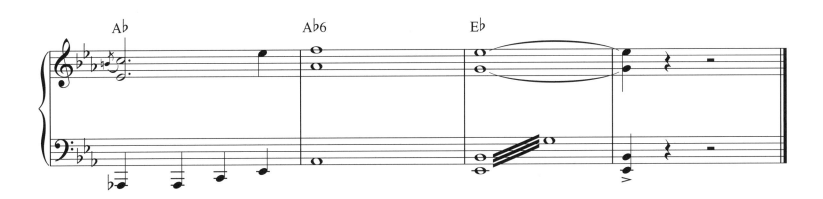

# LA RONDE

By JOHN LEWIS

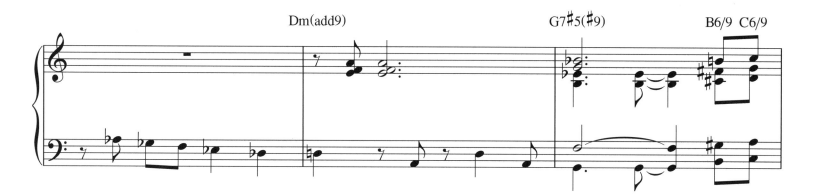

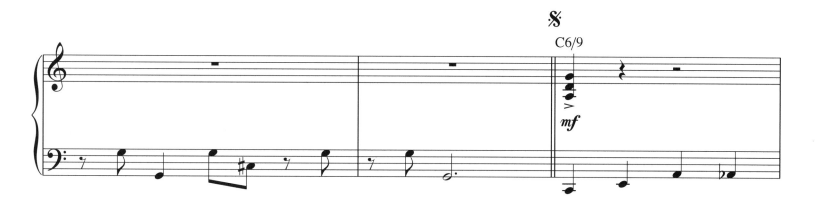

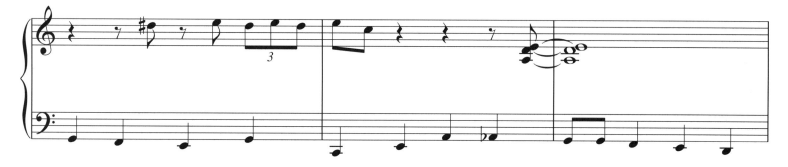

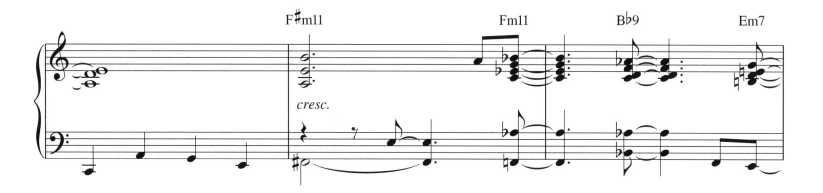

**Fine**

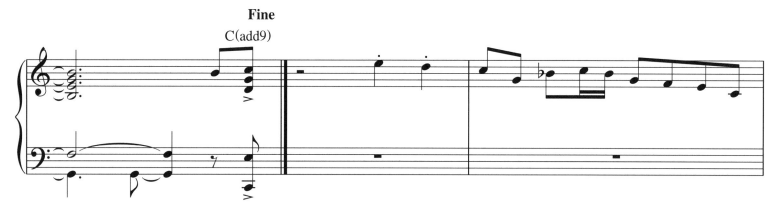

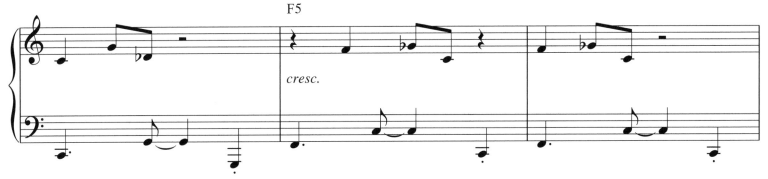

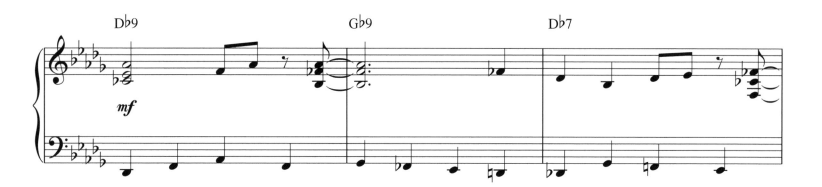

# THE QUEEN'S FANCY

By JOHN LEWIS

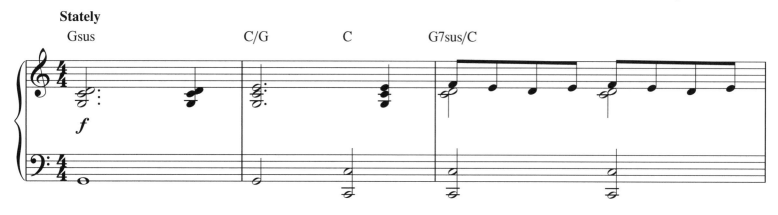

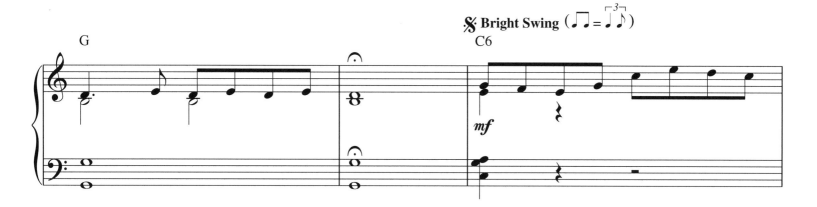

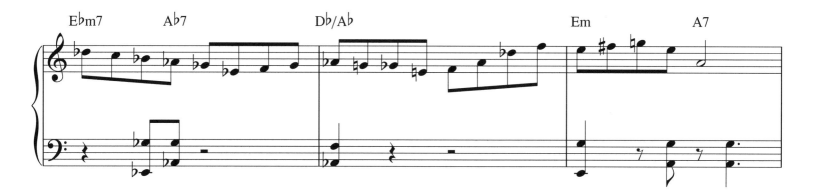

63

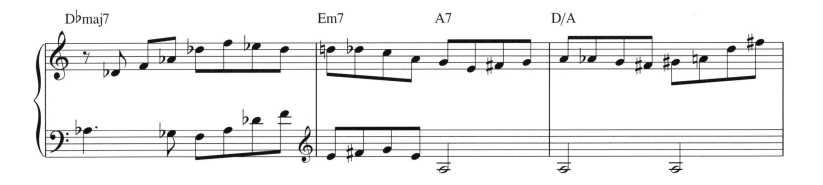

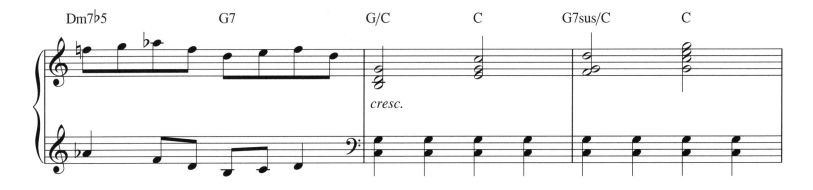

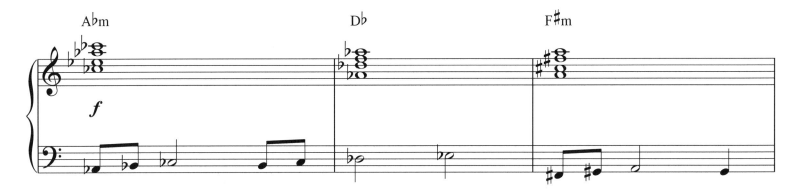

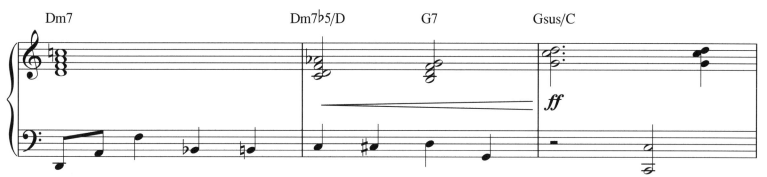

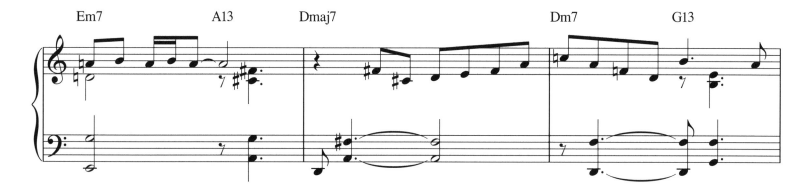

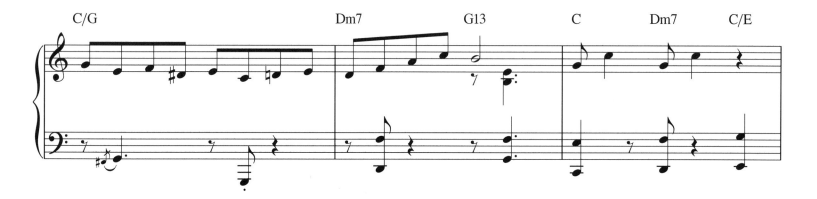

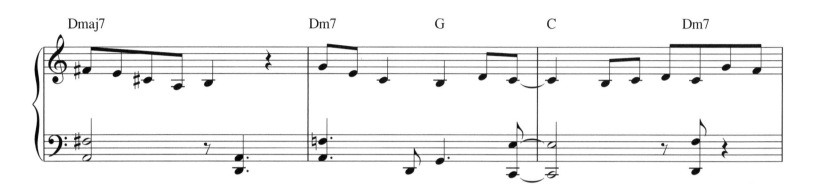

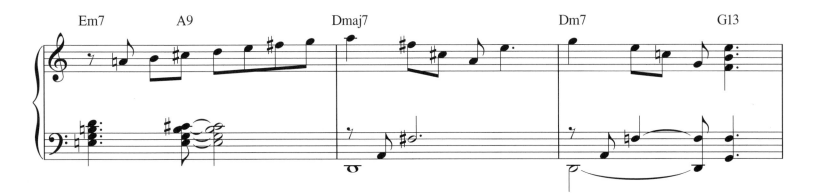

**Even eighths**

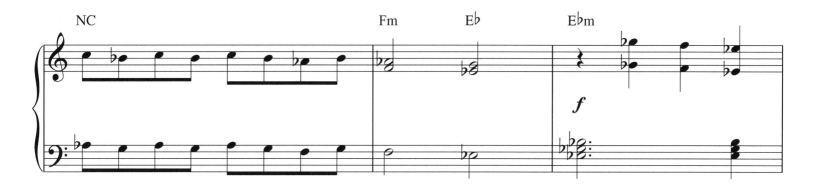

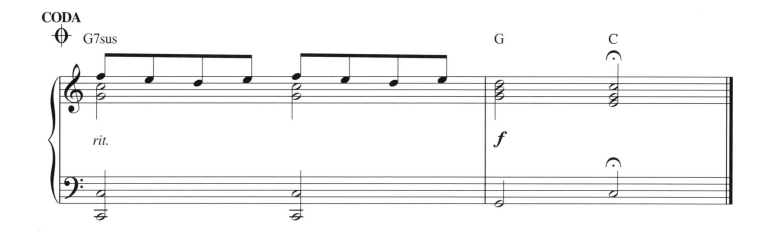

# REUNION BLUES

By MILT JACKSON

**Medium Swing**

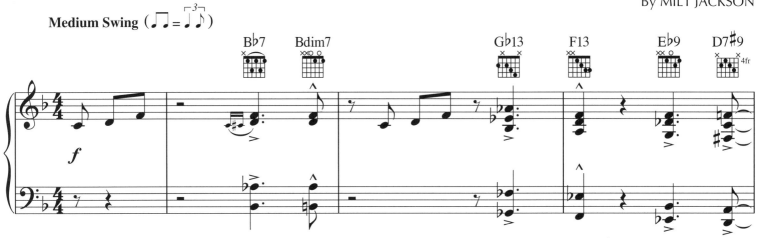

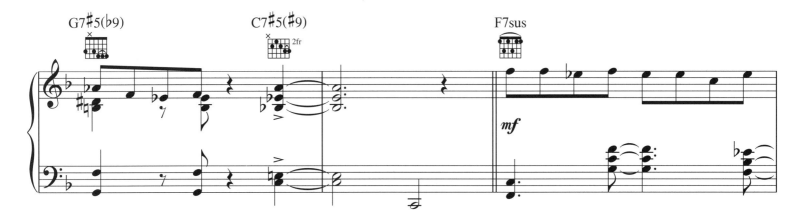

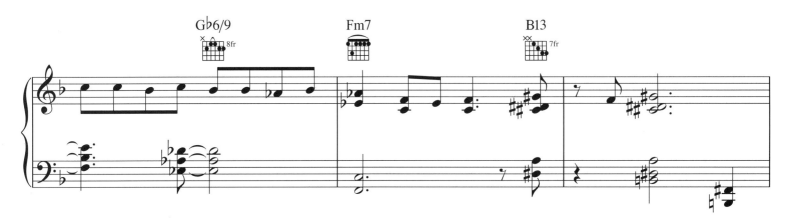

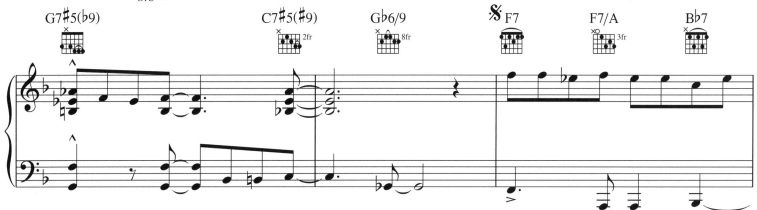

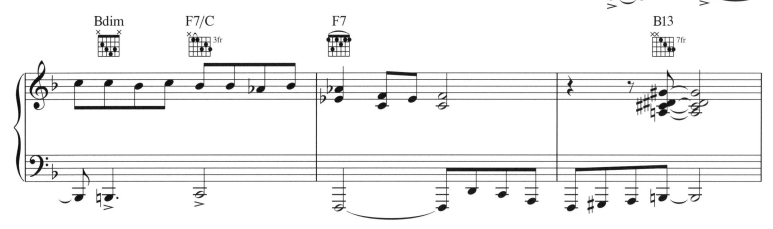

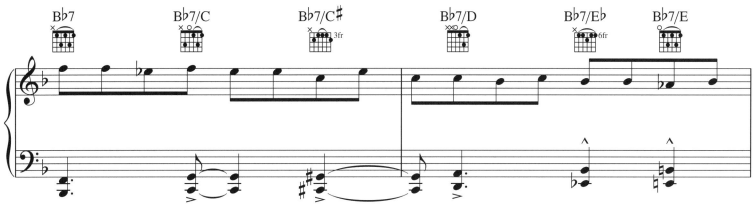

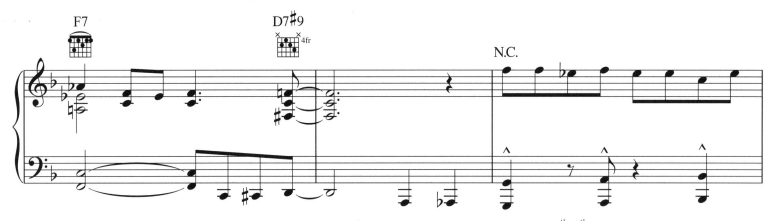

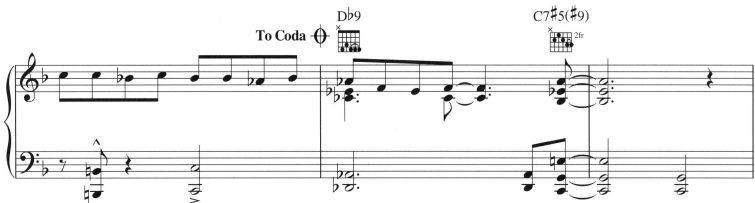

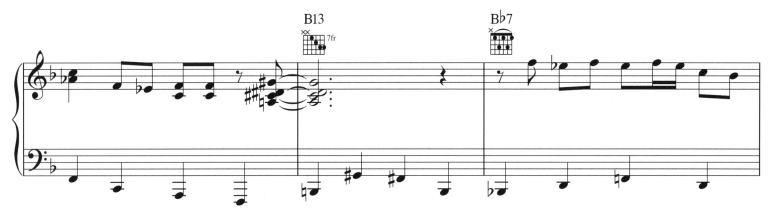

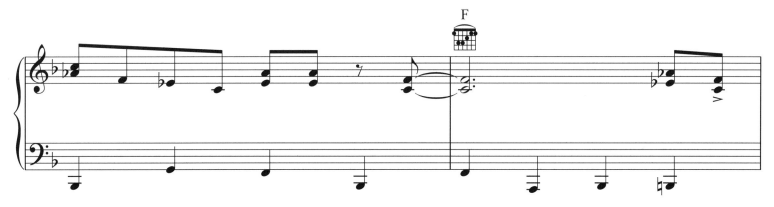

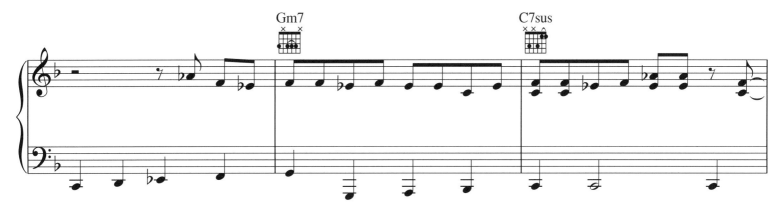

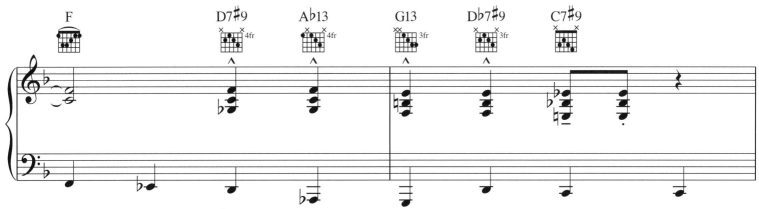

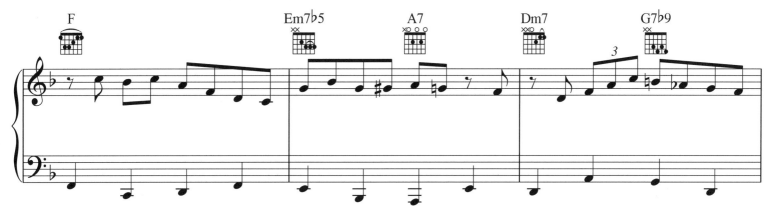

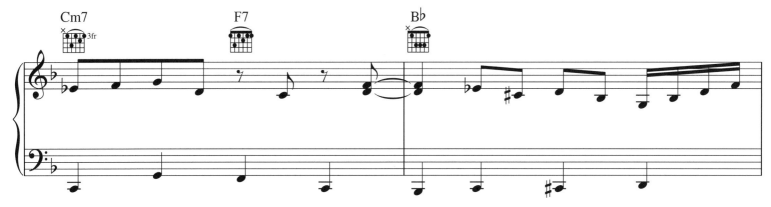

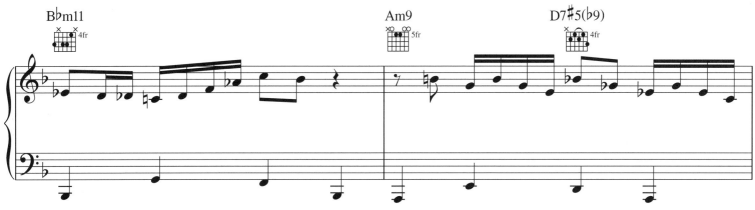

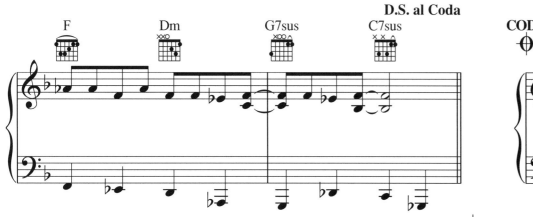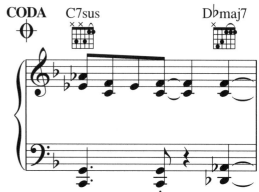

**D.S. al Coda**

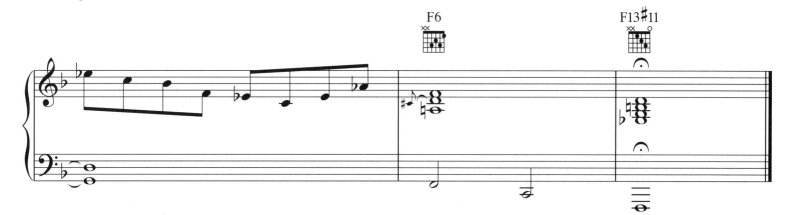

# SKATING IN CENTRAL PARK

By JOHN LEWIS

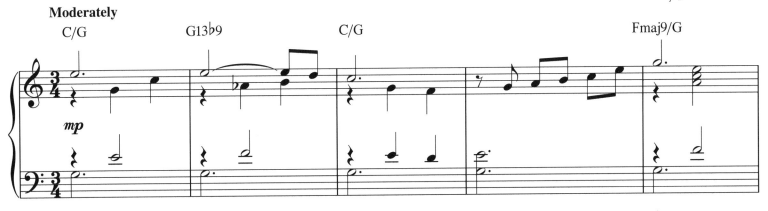

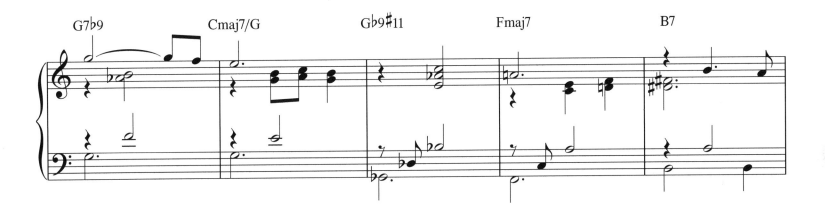

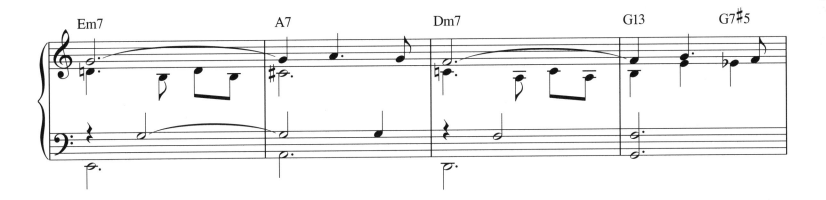

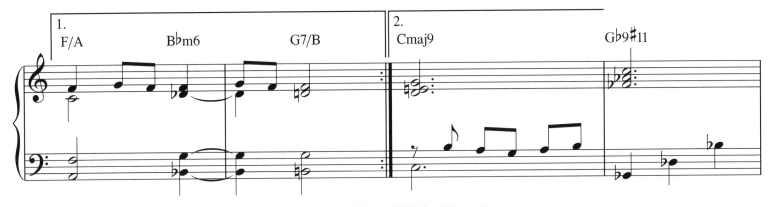

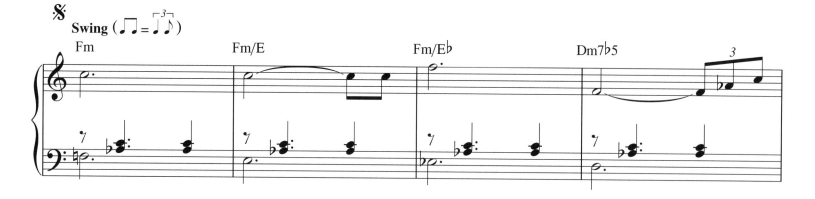

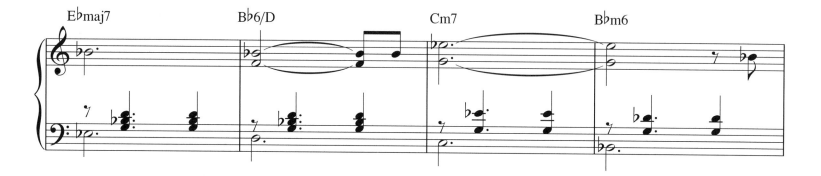

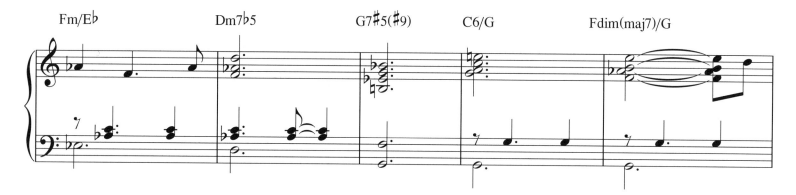

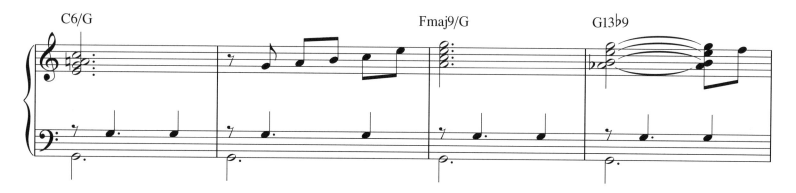

**To Coda** ⊕

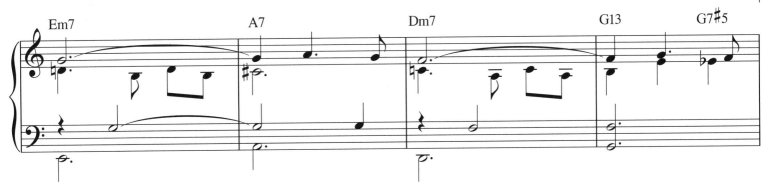

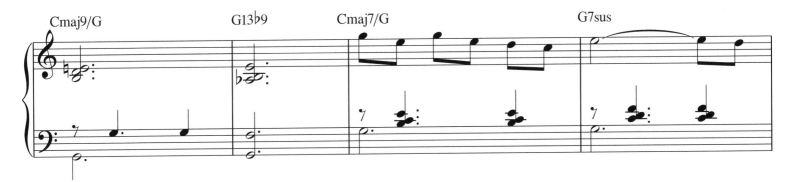

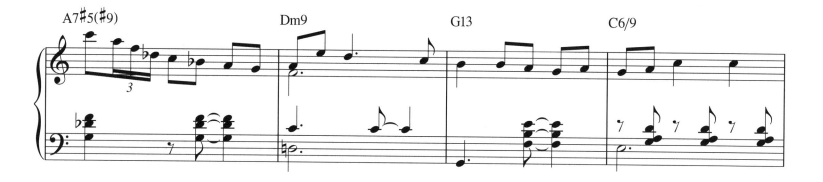

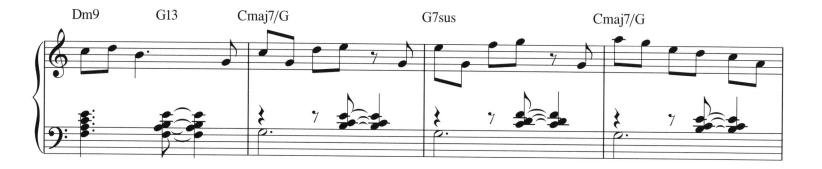

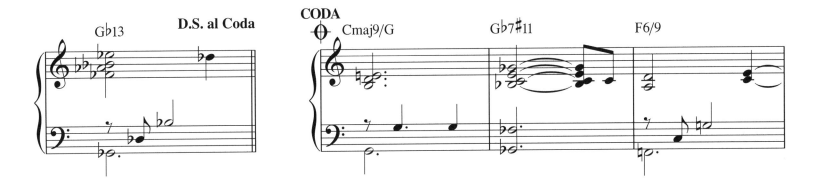

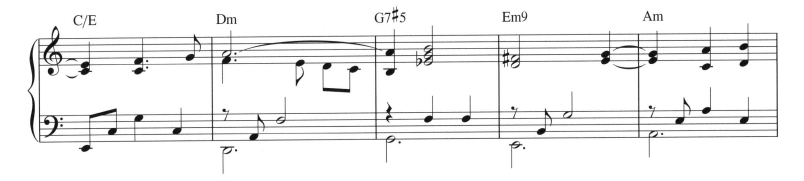

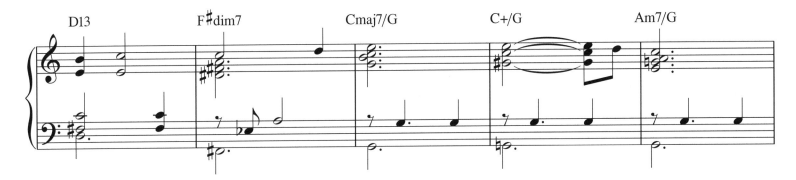

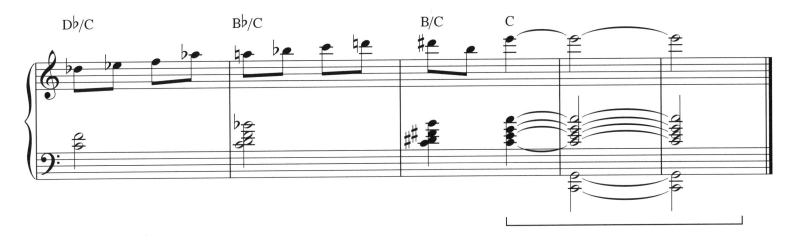

# A SOCIAL CALL

By JOHN LEWIS

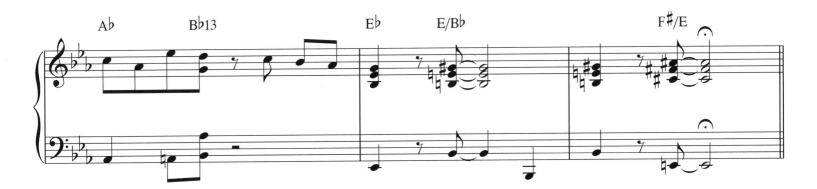

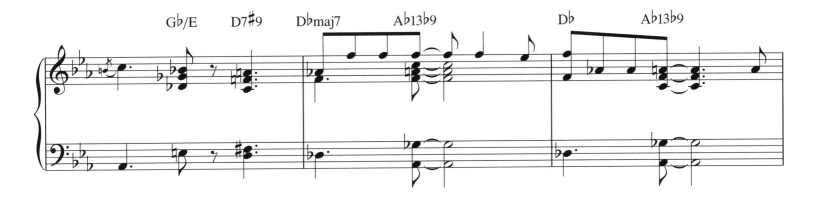

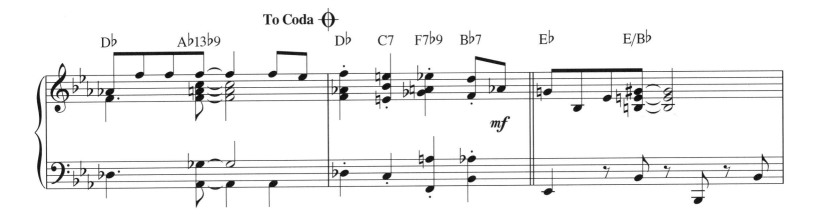

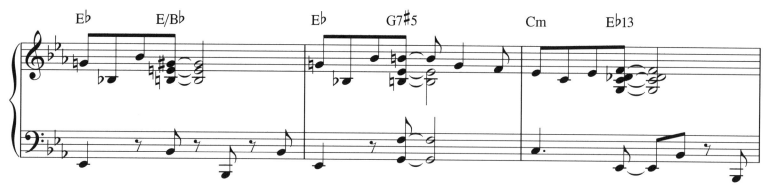

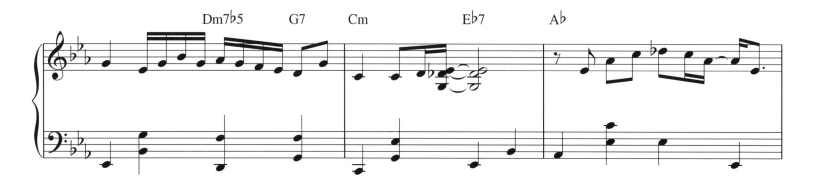

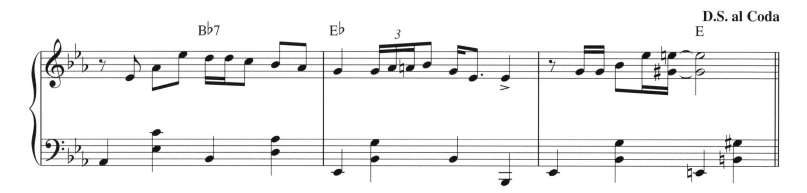

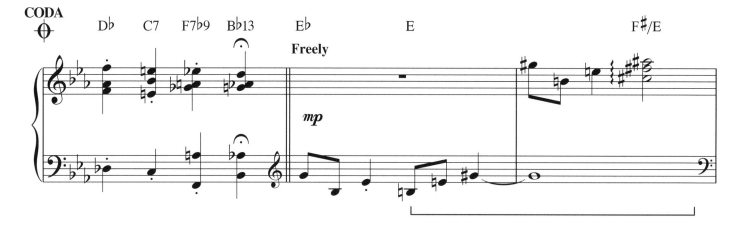

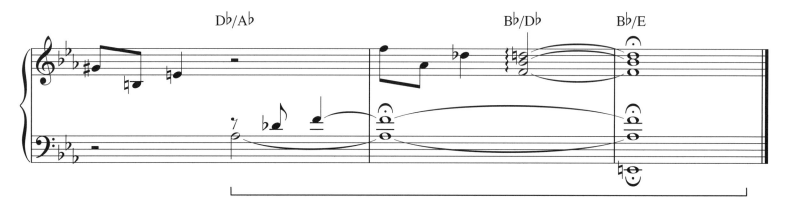

# VENDÔME

By JOHN LEWIS

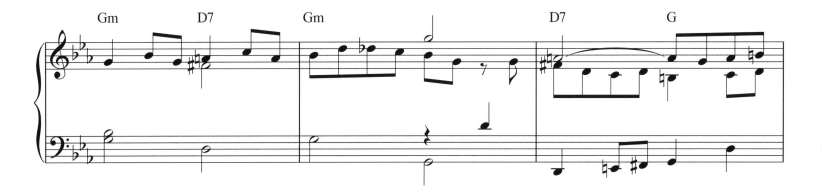

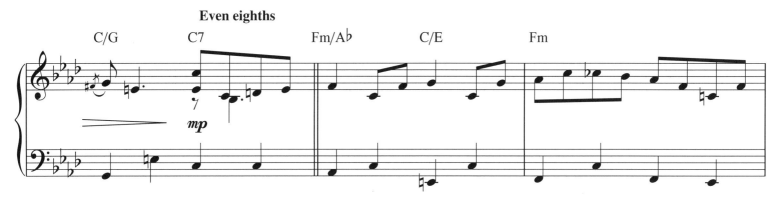

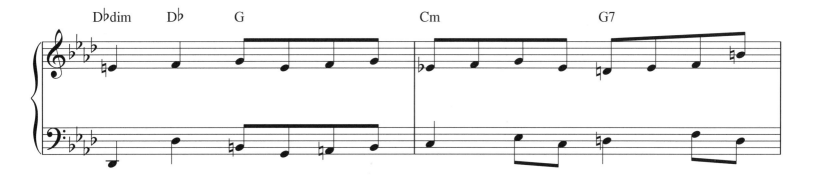

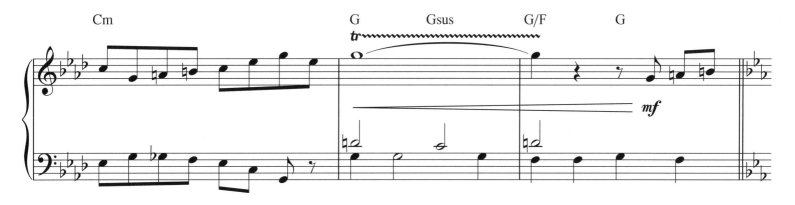

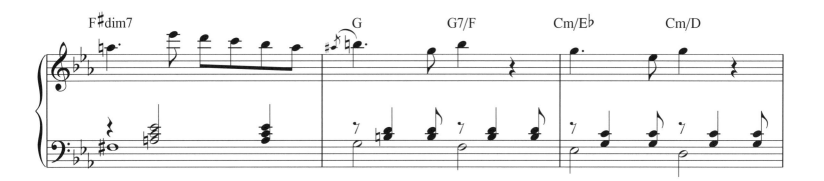

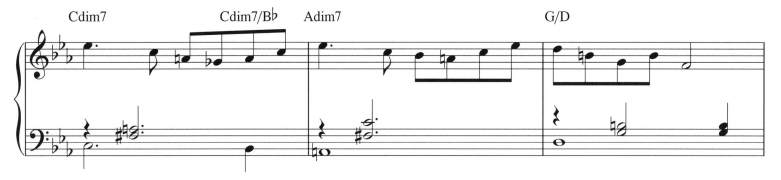

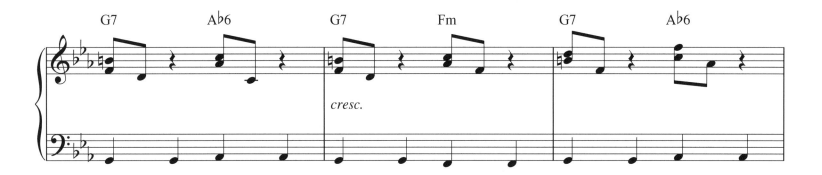

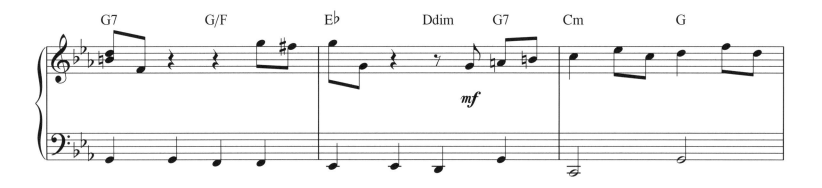

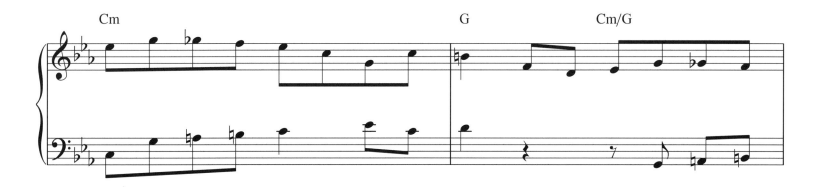

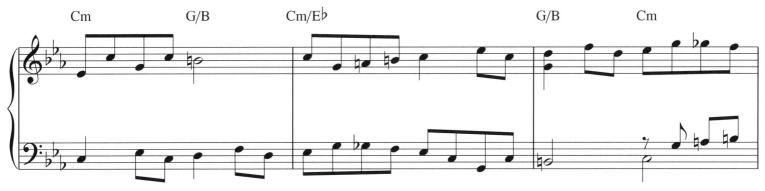

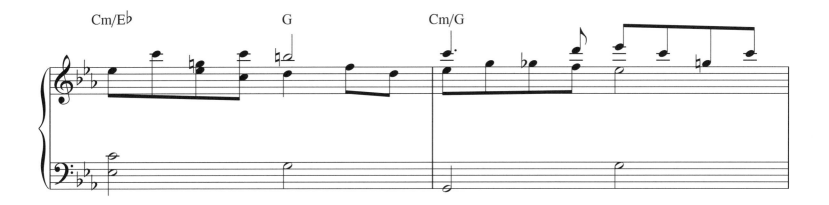

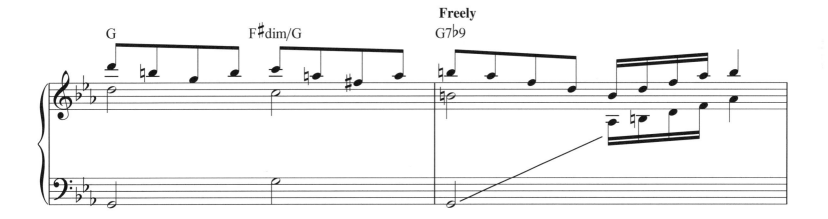

# TEARS FROM THE CHILDREN
## adapted from Prelude VIII, WTC I, J.S. Bach

By JOHN LEWIS

**Lento moderato**

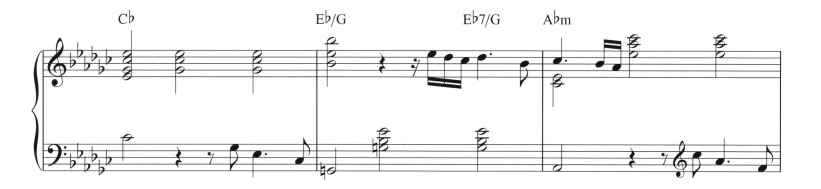

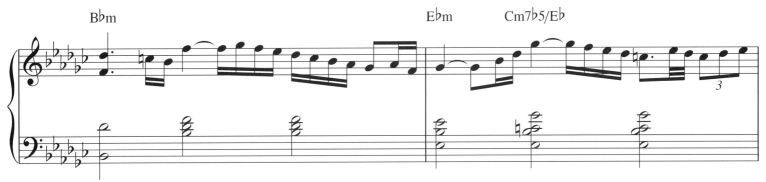

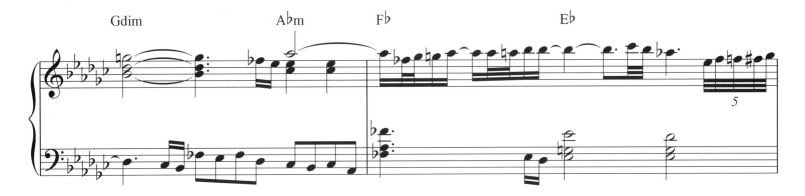

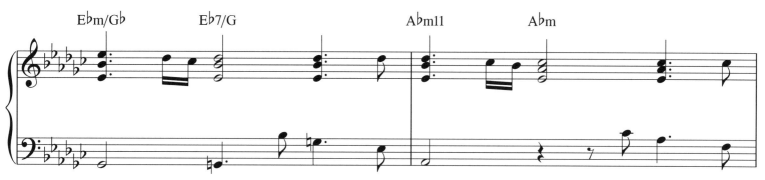

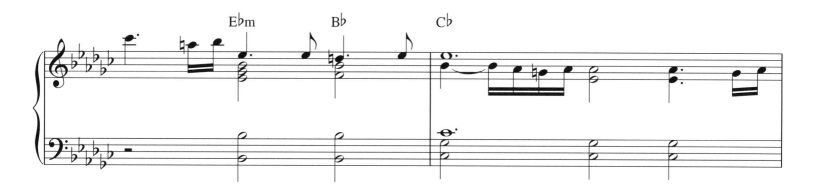

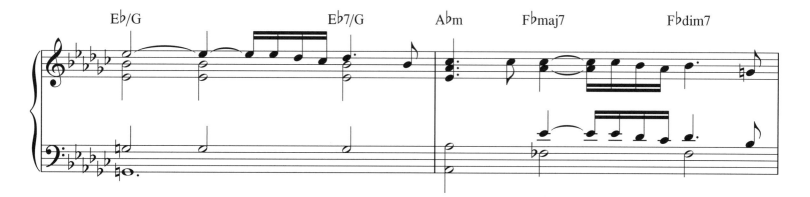

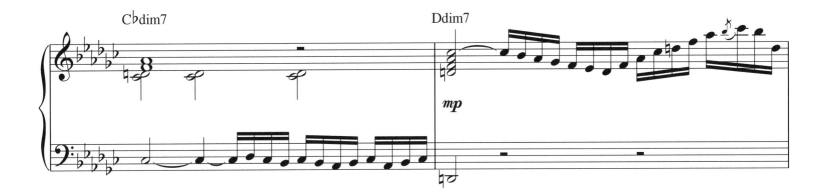

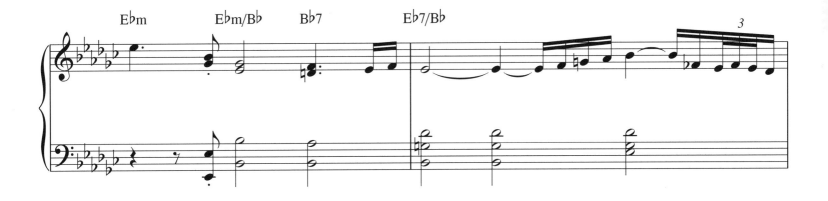

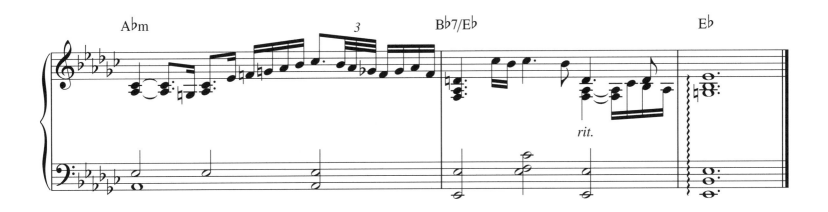

# TWO DEGREES EAST, THREE DEGREES WEST

By JOHN LEWIS

Medium Swing

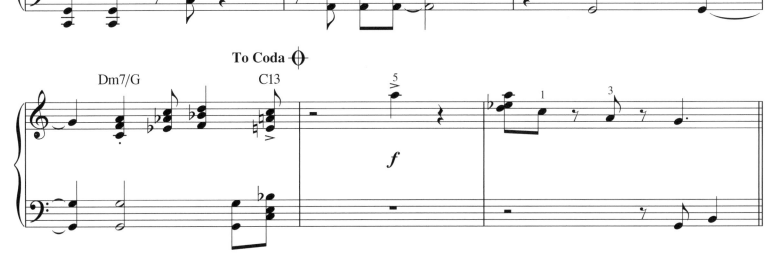

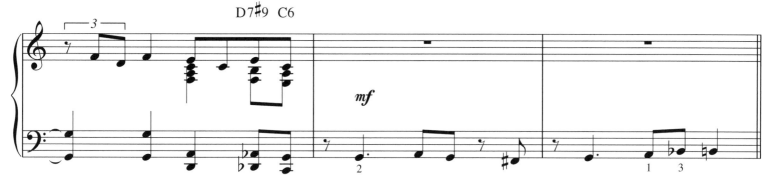

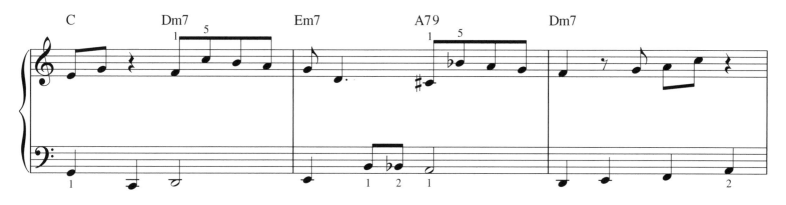

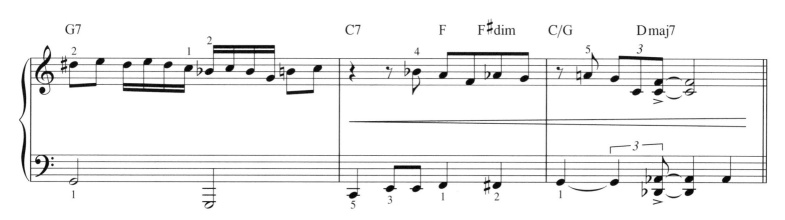

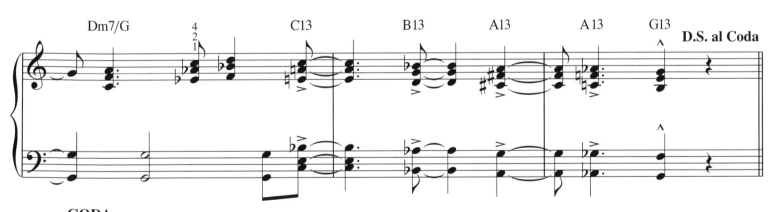